Visual ⊕ Explorers

Machines

BARRON'S

First edition for the United States, its territories and dependencies, and Canada published in 2017 by Barron's Educational Series, Inc.

All inquiries should be addressed to:
Barron's Educational Series, Inc.
250 Wireless Blvd.
Hauppauge, New York 11788
www.barronseduc.com

ISBN: 978-1-4380-1083-0
Library of Congress Control Number: 2017941030

Date of Manufacture: July 2017
Manufactured by: Toppan Leefung Printing Co., Ltd., Shenzhen, China

9 8 7 6 5 4 3 2 1

Photo credits:
Image credits: (t) top, (c) center, (b) bottom, (l) left, (r) right, FF (Fact file)

Airbus Industries – p17 (bl). **Alamy** – p7 (cl) Classic Image, (tcr) Everett Collection Historical. **Andrew Brookes/National Physical Laboratory** – p27 (bl). **Atlantis Submarines** – p15 (tcr). **BAE Systems** – p22 (br). **Boeing** – p23 (trc). **CERN** – FC (bcl). p26 (main). **Flickr** – BC (tl). p13 (tr) Marcela Terra. p20 (cl) Richard. p25 (tcr) Civil Engineering Discoveries. p29 (cl) walter delbono. **Freedom Ship International** – p15 (bl). **Hyundai Motor Company** – p13 (br). **International Space Station (ISS)** – p19 (tr), (tcr), bcr). **Liebherr** – p25 (bl). **Lotus CARS Ltd** – p13 (bl). **Mercedes-Benz Cars** – p11 (cl). p13 (cl). **NASA** – p18 (main), (bl). p19 (tl), (cl), (bl). p23 (bcr). p27 (trc) Ames/Farid Salama. **Public domain** – p4 (main). p7 (tcr), (bcr). p8 (cl). p9 (bl) AlbanyGroup Archive, (tl, tc, tr). p11 (bl). p12 (bl) Abida Motor Companies. p13 (tcr), p14 (br). p15 (cl) Shell Oil and Gas, (tr) Florence8787. p17 (tl), p17 (tr), (tcr), (bcr) BEA de Havilland, (br). p22 (main). p23 (tl), (bl) Sgt. Sarah Dietz/US Marine Corps, (br) Leonid Faerberg (transport-photo.com). p24 (bl) ALMA (ESO/NAOI/NRAO). p25 (tl), (cl), (tr) Belaz, (bcr) Komatzu, (br) www. GOV.cn. p26 (br) Randy Montoya/Sandia National Laboratories. p27 (tl) Intuitive Surgical Inc, (tr) Katrin Heitmann et al/DOE's Argonne National Laboratory, (bcr) National Hurricane Centre/NOAA, (br). p28 (cl). p29 (tl) TedColes, (tr) Local Motors, (tcr) Lance Abernathy, (bcr) Open Bionics, (br) BigRep 3D Printers. p31 (tl) DreamWorld, Brisbane, (bl), (bc). **Rolls-Royce plc** – p17 (cl). **Sauter Design** – p15 (tl). **Science Photo Library** – p5 (tl) Science, Industry and Business Library/New York Library. p7 (bl) Christian Jegou Publiphoto Diffusion, (br). p9 (tcr) LOC/Science Source, (brc), (br) W.W. Austin. p10 (cl) Cordelia Molloy. p13 (tl) WAYHOME STUDIO. p20 (main) Library of Congress. p21 (cl) Sheila Terry. p28 (main) Christian Darkin. **Shutterstock** – FC (main) SH PHOTOCREO Michal Bednarek, (bl) cyo bo, (bcr) FabrikaSimf, (br) Martin Lisner. BC (tcl–tr) OlegSam, maradon 333, Dmitry Laudin. p1 LevanteMedia. p2–3 Andrew Haddon. p4 (bl) Waj. p5 (cl) maradon 333, (bl) Morphant Creation, (tr–br) Izf, Andris Tkacenko, aastock, Stanislaw Mikulski. p6 (main) Mitch Gunn, (bl) Viktor Gladkov. p7 (tl) Lagui. p8 (main) Dmitry Laudin. p9 (cl) Morphant Creation. p10 (main) cristiano barni. p11 (tl) Angyalosi Beata, (cr) Iaroslav Neliubov. p12 (main) cyo bo. p15 (bcr) Leonid Andronov, (br) Leonid Eremeychuk. p16 (br) Arsgera. p20 (tl) Everett Historical. p21 (bl) Bplanet, (tr) P. Kamput, (trc) OlegSam, (brc) Fabian Faber, (br) lightmood. p23 (cl) photowrzesien, (tr) Jose Gil. p24 (main) Martin Lisner. p29 (bl) Alex_Traksel, (bc) FabrikaSimf. p30 (main) X-RAY pictures, (cl) Dreamsgate Pictures. p31 (tr–br) LittleDogKorat, AForlenza, Weigelstein, Syda Productions. p32 (br) Jeroenbfoto. **Tesla Inc** – p27 (cl). **Toyota Motors** – p19 (bcr). **Triton Submarines LCC** – p14 (main). **Venturi** – p13 (bcr). **Yves Rossy** – p15 (main). **Zollner Electronics** – p31 (cl).

Introduction

From the moment our ancestors first fashioned rocks into hunting spears and axe heads, machines have made our lives easier, more efficient, and more fun. Scientists have continued to innovate since the development of the wheel and axle, creating machines that help us harvest food, complete chores, fight in world conflicts, entertain others, and travel as far as the depths of space. Whether a simple tool or a complex robot, machines play a crucial role in shaping and powering the world we live in today.

Contents

Read on to find out more about machines and the jobs they do...

Simple machines

Simple machines have contributed to the **survival** of the human species. A wooden **stick** made digging a well or lifting vegetables from the **ground** easier for early humans, and a hammerstone could chip sharp edges into a **rock** that in turn could chisel a point on a hunting spear or a blade on an axe head. The **humans** that first made stone tools, some **1.6–3.4 million** years ago, are called *Homo habilis*, meaning **"handy man."** *Homo habilis* used muscles to "power" the **machines** that made **scavenging**, hunting, and shelter-building easier.

Facts and figures

Wheel and axle development

Rolling log
This was a forerunner of the wheel and axle in that it made moving things over a distance easier. A log, felled and trimmed using stone tools, was placed under an object. When the log was rolled, the object moved with it.

Potter's wheel
In 3,500 BCE, the wheel and axle were used in pottery-making. Making a pottery wheel required metal tools, which first appeared only 1,500 years earlier.

Transport
The first wheel-and-axle transport was a cart in 3,200 BCE. But wheeled transport was not an overnight success, and camels continued to rule the trade routes for another 600 years. Meanwhile, the wheel and axle were used for milling and irrigation purposes.

The 4,500-year-old Standard of Ur is one of the earliest depictions of the wheel and axle

Did you know?

To move blocks weighing up to 69.4 US tons (63 metric tons), the Egyptian pyramid builders used ramps and rolling logs, which are early forms of the lever and the wheel and axle.

The **wheel** and **axle** in **combination** was the **most** **important** **simple machine** ever **invented.**

Input and output

A tool or machine is only useful (gives a mechanical advantage) if it changes a small input of force into a larger output.

What is a force?

When one object pushes or pulls on another object it is a force. A jack turns a small force—the effort used by your muscles—into a much stronger force.

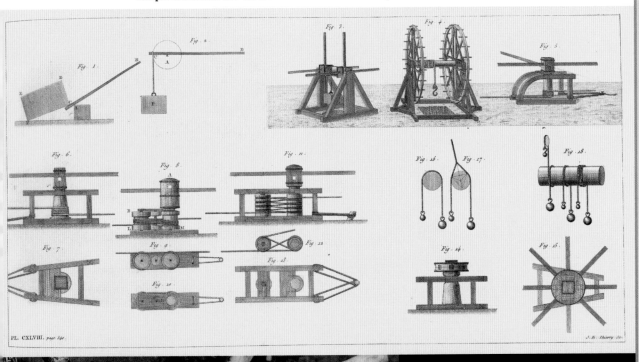

PL. CXLVIII. *page 340.*   J. E. Thierry. *sc.*

Fact file

Simple everyday machines

We use simple machines every day. To open a can of beans, for example, you pull (apply force) on the ring pull (a lever).

Wheel and axle
A rotation of the axle—a small "wheel"—makes a large rotation of the wheel in skateboards and more.

Lever
A claw hammer is a lever. A small downward force, which pivots on a fulcrum, creates a large upward force.

Inclined plane
This angled surface, as seen in a ladder and ramp, makes it easier to move an object to a higher level.

Wedge
When force is applied to a wedge, such as an axe head, nail, or plow, it penetrates another object.

What is a machine?

A successful machine does work using minimum effort to achieve maximum effect, making work easier. The simple machines are the wheel and axle, lever, and inclined plane. There is also the pulley (a wheel on a axle), wedge (two inclined planes), and screw (an inclined plane).

Prehistoric tools

When Stone Age people hammered a stone against a flint to shape it into an axe, they were using a tool to do work. The hammer stone was the machine. The world's first toolkit, the Oldowan, is 2.5 million years old. It consists of hammer stones and sharp-edged, stone flake-cutting tools.

A stone axe head is a wedge, a simple machine for chopping wood

Archimedes' screw

Archimedes (287–212 BCE) was a Greek inventor. He proposed the principles of simple machines and mechanical advantage. With a lever in his hand, Archimedes knew he could "move the Earth." The Archimedes' screw is an inclined plane wrapped around a shaft, and when turned moves water uphill!

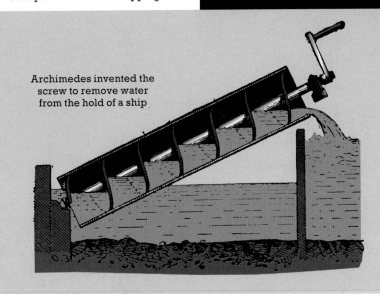

Archimedes invented the screw to remove water from the hold of a ship

5

Complex machines

Complex or compound machines are a combination of simple machines working together. A gear is a toothed wheel on an **axle**—a simple machine—but link gears together in a **chain** and you get a **compound** machine, where the output force of one becomes the input force for the next. The first complex **machine** was used by the **Chinese** to carve grooves into jade rings around 2,500 years ago. **Pre-industrial** complex machines were **powered** by humans, animals, wind, and water, but modern machines chiefly rely on **fossil** fuel energy.

Did you know?

None of Leonardo da Vinci's complex machines were built in his lifetime, but the genius of this 15th-century inventor is evident in the models, like this crane, based on da Vinci's plans.

Even without brakes and gears, a track bike is a highly complex machine

Complex machines take even *more effort* out of difficult and dangerous tasks.

Huygens' clock

Huygens' 1656 pendulum clock made timekeeping precise. Its swinging pendulum and refined machining lost only 15 seconds in a day. Earlier clocks lost 15 minutes!

First true piano

In 1709, Cristoflori replaced a string-plucking mechanism with a hammer, creating a piano that could play "loud and soft."

Feared machine

The Chinese invented the trebuchet, or catapult, in 300 BCE, and it reached Europe 800 years later. The throwing arm is a simple lever. When the counterweight is dropped, the lever accelerates in an arc, propelling the missile from its sling. A trebuchet could fire a 110-pound (50-kg) missile 984 feet (300 m).

Fact file

Weird complex machines

These machines were once cutting-edge, combining and innovating simple machines in order to make the next must-have device.

1678: Firefighting
Handles were pumped by hand to propel the water from the tank onto the fire. This is the first fire engine.

On the farm

Since humans had first cultivated crops, harvesting had been done by hand. When the first machines (reapers) appeared in the 1800s they revolutionized agriculture. What once took a laborer a week to do could be done in an hour by a machine.

Hot off the press

Japan, Korea, and China had types of printing presses since the 8th century, but Johannes Gutenberg invented a mechanized process that transferred the ink on the type to the paper. His 1450s machine made it possible to mass-produce books cheaply and quickly. Gutenberg's press is rated among the world's most important inventions.

An 1828 reaping machine was pushed by a pair of horses

1786: Gymnasticon
Consisting of flywheels and treadles, this wooden "cross trainer" exercised every part of the body.

1818: Velocipede
Also known as a dandy horse, the rider walked or ran to propel this forerunner of the bicycle.

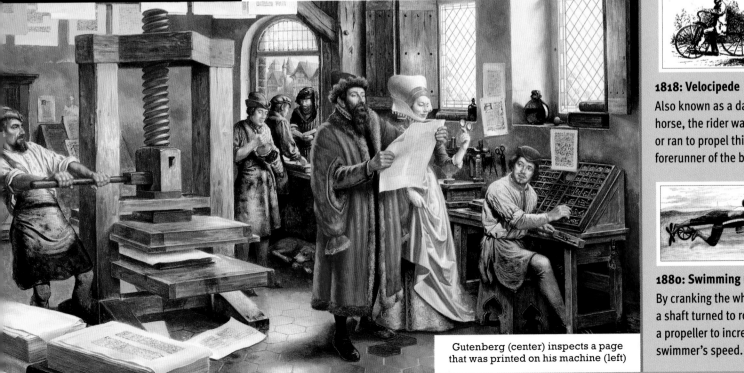

Gutenberg (center) inspects a page that was printed on his machine (left)

1880: Swimming machine
By cranking the wheels, a shaft turned to rotate a propeller to increase a swimmer's speed.

The age of steam

Steam **power** turned the wheels of an agricultural and industrial revolution (1740–1840). Once practical steam-powered **engines** appeared, they were used to **improve** the extraction of coal from mines in order to feed the **boilers** of the engines that quickly **dominated** factory floors, farms, and railway tracks. Steam-powered **machines** increased productivity. They meant that factories could be located away from the **rivers** that had driven milling and textile industry **waterwheels**. Europe's steam age ended in **1914** with the arrival of the internal combustion engine.

Facts and figures

How a piston steam engine works

Stage 1
First, a fuel, such as wood, coal, or coke, is burned in a firebox to produce heat.

Stage 2
Water in the boiler, which sits over or near the firebox, is heated by the burning fuel to make steam.

Stage 3
The steam is piped into a cylinder. Inside the cylinder is a piston.

Stage 4
The steam moves the piston, causing other components to move.

Stage 5
When the piston has moved, a vent is opened to release the steam. The piston moves back down the cylinder.

Stage 6
The vent is closed and steam builds up in the cylinder, moving the piston on another cycle.

Did you know?

The first steam-powered machine was Hero's aerolipile in the 1st century CE. When the water-filled sphere was heated, steam jetted from nozzles, causing the sphere to spin!

While this steam locomotive powered along, a stoker would be feeding the fire with coal

Using only water and coal, a steam locomotive could travel at 99.4 miles (160 kilometers) per hour.

Steam rollers

The first of these heavy vehicles appeared in 1866. They were an immediate success because they cut construction costs.

Edison's power plant

Thomas Edison built the world's first commercial power plant in 1882. Its electricity generators were powered by high-speed steam engines.

Steam's big three

Thomas Savery built the first steam-powered machine, "an engine to raise water by fire." Thomas Newcomen and James Watt improved on Savery's design, using pistons, cylinders, and a separate condenser. Watt's reliable engines could power any sort of factory, no matter what it produced.

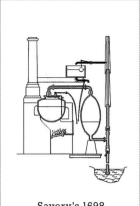

Savery's 1698 "Miner's Friend" pumped water from mines

Newcomen's 1712 steam engine moved an arm up and down

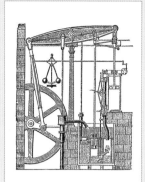

Watt's 1769 "Old Bess" steam engine produced rotary motion

Stephenson's "Rocket" reached a top speed of 23.6 miles (38 km) per hour

A replica of the *Clermont*, a long-distance paddlewheel steamboat

On the tracks

Richard Trevithick built the first steam locomotive in 1804, but it was George Stephenson's developments in 1829 that inspired steam locomotion for the next 150 years. Both engineers used high-pressure steam, but Stephenson's innovations to the boiler made his "Rocket" more efficient, powerful, and reliable, and faster.

On the water

Robert Fulton's *Clermont* steamed along New York's Hudson River in 1811, starting commercial steamboat passenger and cargo transport. The *Clermont* was powered by a Watt's steam engine, and its wooden paddlewheels were 15 feet (4.6 m) in diameter.

Fact file

Steam power

Inventors were enthralled by steam power, but not all their labors produced useful machines. Some were simply useless!

1843: Aerial carriage
This 1843 monoplane may have worked if its very heavy steam engine had produced enough power.

10–70 CE: Door opener
When heated water flowed into a pot and increased its weight, the pot pulled a rope that opened a door.

1771: Car
Cugnot's car had the first automobile accident, and its steam engine had to be relit every 15 minutes.

1867–1869: Velocipede
Water, hand-pumped from the saddle, was heated by a firebox under the boiler between the wheels.

Machines under power

In addition to **steam** power, machines work under the power of water, **wind**, solar energy, fossil fuels, nuclear energy, and battery. Some machines, like **clockwork** toys, use the energy released from a **coiled** spring, and water turns the turbines in hydroelectric stations. An **F1 car** can use its electric recovery system (ERS) to retrieve braking power from the combustion engine to **boost** its **speed**. What is surprising is that inventors were designing machines that used sustainable **energy**, like wind and solar, hundreds of years before our use of fossil fuels became a **global** issue.

Facts and figures

Energy timeline

2,000 BCE: Coal is used for heating in China.	**1870:** Petroleum is the main energy source in the US.
200 BCE: Natural gas is used in China; water power is used in Europe.	**1888:** Windmills produce electricity.
1st century CE: China refines oil for energy.	**1890:** Vegetable oil powers an engine.
10th century CE: Persia uses windmills.	**1927:** Wind turbines produce electricity.
1700s: Whale oil is used as a fuel.	**1950s:** Natural gas is a major fuel.
1860: Solar power is used.	**2012:** Coal makes 40% of global electricity.

Did you know?

A wind-up radio will operate for up to 55 minutes when fully charged, but to power up a laptop computer for 1 minute would require 10 minutes of hand-aching winding!

An F1 car is the most sophisticated and complex machine on the road

Battery power

Wet and dry cell batteries were invented in the 1880s, but no portable power source has gone quite as far as the batteries on the International Space Station have.

Nuclear power

The heat from a nuclear reactor produces steam that drives a turbine linked to a generator, which then makes electricity.

Watermills were once widespread in Europe

Watermills

In the 1800s, there were over 20,000 watermills in Britain and Europe. A wheel fitted with paddles or blades is placed along a stretch of flowing or falling water. As the water hits the blades, the wheel turns its axle, which in turn drives the belts and pulleys on another machine.

ICE and Daimler

An internal combustion engine (ICE) turns chemical energy in the fuel to mechanical energy. An ICE can be small yet still provide lots of power. At an engine's core are pistons, which move up and down the cylinders. These drive a crankshaft and flywheel, which powers the gears and wheels.

It took only **15 years** for the **internal combustion engine** to **clear London streets** of **horses.**

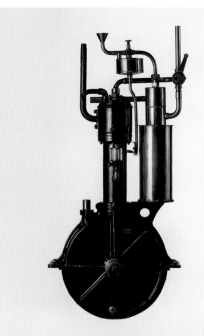
Gottlieb Daimler's groundbreaking 1884 "Grandfather Clock" engine

A computer-generated image of a modern V8 internal combustion engine

Life of an engine

There are 80,000 components in an F1 car. In races, its engine is replaced every 2 hours.

First Benz car

Karl Benz (1844–1929) built the first car, the *Motorwagon*, which was powered by an internal combustion engine.

Abel Pifre's solar-powered printing press being demonstrated in Paris

The power of the Sun

In the 1860s, Augustin Mouchot turned solar energy, collected in a concave mirror, into steam power to drive a machine. Ahead of his time, he believed that coal would run out. Abel Pifre, Mouchot's assistant, built a solar-powered printing press that could produce 500 copies an hour.

Land vehicles

When you think of land vehicles, **cars** and trucks come to mind, but there is endless **variety**. Some vehicles get you to school while others can **traverse** the Antarctic. There are even machines that take the walking out of walking, like **escalators**, moving footpaths, and autonomous driving **cars**. While some vehicles transport thousands of people, others break **speed** records. Crucial inventions in the history of land vehicles were the **wheel** and **axle**, internal combustion engine, steam engine, and Henry Ford's **mass** production assembly line—which is a machine itself!

Maglev trains don't have wheels or axles— they **float** on a magnetic field over the **tracks**.

Did you know?

This prototype electric bus, which runs on tracks, allows two lanes of traffic to flow under it. Passengers would board the "tunnel bus" from elevated road-side platforms.

China's Shanghai Maglev is the world's fastest train, speeding at 310.7 miles (500 kilometers) per hour

Tube to Beijing!

Capsules floating on magnetic fields inside vacuum tubes could travel from New York to Beijing in 2 hours. At 4,039 miles (6,500 kilometers) per hour, it would be space travel on Earth!

Electric scooters

The first electric motorcycle of 1895 had a top speed of 34.8 miles (56 km) per hour. The current record is 196.4 miles (316 km) per hour.

Electric-assist gives mountain bikes a top speed of 15.5 miles (25 km) per hour

Land speed record breakers

The first land speed record of 39 miles (63 km) per hour was in an electric car, the Jeantaud, in 1898. Below are current speed freaks.

JCB Dieselmax

On the Bonneville Salt Flats in Utah, in 2006 this diesel-fueled car did 350.1 miles (563.418 km) per hour.

Thrust SCC

Two fighter jet engines powered this supersonic car to 762.4 miles (1227 km) per hour on October 15, 1997.

Venturi Buckeye Bullet 3

This electric- and lithium-battery–powered, 36 foot (11 m) car hit 341.7 miles (549.9 km) an hour in 2016.

Pedal power

There are an estimated 1 billion bikes on the world's roads—equal to the number of cars. Early wooden-wheeled, iron-framed bicycles were known as "boneshakers" for good reasons, but modern bikes are smooth riding and lightweight machines—some with computer sensors—where pedal power can be aided by electric or solar motors.

Driverless cars

Also known as autonomous vehicles (AVs), they "see" their surroundings with optical camera sensors and lasers, which can take 1.3 million readings per second. Under the bonnet, AVs look like other cars, but some have no steering wheel or floor pedals.

The front seats in the Mercedes-Benz F 015 AV rotate, so there is no need to even watch the road

Inspired ice vehicle

This vehicle on skids was designed for the world's harshest environment—the Antarctic. It runs on biofuel (from plant material), is propeller driven, and its radar detects crevasses and the thickness of the ice. The ice vehicle was tested in a 2,485.5-mile (4,000-km)-long trans-Antarctic expedition.

The Concept Ice Vehicle was developed in 2009

Hyundai IONIQ Hybrid

This modified electric and petroleum production car reached 157.8 miles (253.9 km) per hour in 2016.

Marine machines

The first water-going **craft** were dugout canoes—tree trunks, up to 59 feet (18 meters) long, **hollowed** out with stone-age tools. The ancient Egyptians and Chinese added **sails**, so exploration, trade, and even **"ferry"** services started. Boats grew in size, oceans were crossed, territories were discovered, and **naval** battles were won and lost. Tired of being *on* the **water**, submarines appeared in the 1700s, but mostly sank. Weary of waiting for fair winds, **steamships** cruised in the 1800s. **Mariners** in small wooden ships mapped the world that is now criss-crossed by over 50,000 mammoth merchant **ships**.

Facts and figures

Cruise ship giants

Harmony of the Seas
Length: 1,187.7 ft (362 m)
Width: 214.9 ft (65.5 m)
Passengers: 6,360
Crew: 2,100
Features: surf pool and 10-story dry slide.

Allure of the Seas and Oasis of the Seas
Length: 1,184.4 ft (361 m)
Width: 214.9 ft (65.5 m)
Passengers: 6,318
Crew: 2,384
Features: malls powered by solar arrays and an outdoor cinema screen.

Quantum of the Seas
Length: 1,138 ft (347 m)
Width: 134.5 ft (41 m)
Passengers: 4,905
Crew: 1,500
Features: a glass viewing capsule that can be raised 295.3 ft (90 m) above sea level.

Ovation of the Seas
Length: 1,135.2 ft (346 m)
Width: 134.5 ft (41 m)
Passengers: 4,819
Crew: 1,300
Features: skydiving simulator & dodgems.

A Triton submersible at a depth of 3,280 feet (1,000 meters) recorded the first encounter with a giant squid

Submersibles can explore Earth's inner space— its ocean's deepest waters.

Bathing machine

To protect people's modesty at the beach in the 1700s–1800s, this dressing room on wheels was pulled into the sea, then the bather would descend the stairs to the water.

Robot submarine

Unmanned subs are used to explore at great depths or under ice shelves. They are controlled from a mothership.

Did you know?

The largest self-propelled object ever built was the *Seawise Giant*, an ultra-large oil tanker 1,502.6 ft (458 m) long. It could carry over 4 million barrels of oil. It was scrapped in 2009.

Eco-yachts

A 137.8-foot (42-m)-long luxury yacht may cost a lot, but it doesn't have to cost the Earth, as the new eco vessels prove. These yachts are carbon-zero using solar, water, and wind energy to counter fuel usage.

Offshore platform

An offshore platform extracts oil and gas from under the sea. The rig is either fixed to the seafloor or is anchored and floats. It is home to its workers and has to weather 65-ft (20-m) waves. Sakhalin-2, a floating rig, weighs 30,864.7 US tons (28,000 metric tons) and is linked to its refinery by 497.1-mile (800-km)-long pipelines.

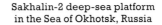
Ocean Empire LSV is an eco-yacht that uses solar, wind, and wave power

Sakhalin-2 deep-sea platform in the Sea of Okhotsk, Russia

A city in the ocean

This floating city, four times the size of the *Queen Mary*, would have an airport, apartments, shops, businesses, banks, parks, schools, cinemas, healthcare, leisure centers, light industry, and hotels. It would travel the world with its 40,000 residents, 10,000 hotel guests, and 20,000 crew.

A computer image of the proposed *Freedom Ship*

Machines take flight

Humans have always looked up to the **skies**, wishing they could soar like **birds**. Inventors initially mimicked birds, flapping themselves airborne on fabric and wooden **wings**. Over following centuries, many **devices** were tried and tested—hot air balloons, gliders, steam-powered craft—but the breakthrough came in **1903** with the **Wright brothers**. That critical event paved the way for an aviation industry where craft got larger and engines **grew** more powerful. Today's commercial aircraft are not bound to **Earth's** skies—they are approaching hypersonic speeds at the doors of **space**.

At **takeoff,** two jet engines produce **thrust** equal to the **power** of 1,500 cars!

Yves "Jetman" Rossy flying his jet engine–powered wing suit, which measures 7.9 feet (2.4 m) across

Did you know?

This microlight has a hang-glider wing, and suspended under it is a trike for up to two passengers. Microlights have an engine and propeller at the rear of the trike.

Flying boat pioneer

In 1914, a flying boat flew across Tampa Bay, Florida. As the first-ever scheduled passenger route, it did the 11-mile (29-km) trip in 11 minutes, flying 6.6 feet (2 m) above the water.

Private aircraft

There are about 20,000 private aircraft in the world. They are owned by individuals, companies, and governments.

The Wright *Flyer* on its history-making flight

Aircraft that made history

Because of their triumphs or disasters, these four aircraft have attained legendary status.

The Hindenburg
In 1937, the hydrogen gas used in this airship ignited, causing 37 deaths, as it moored to its landing mast.

Heavier-than-air flight

The forces of heavier-than-air flight—lift, drag, thrust, and weight—were worked out in 1853, but it was the Wright brothers who first flew a powered heavier-than-air controllable airplane. Their *Flyer* took off from Kitty Hawk in North Carolina, in 1903 and flew for 12 seconds over a distance of 121.4 ft (37 m).

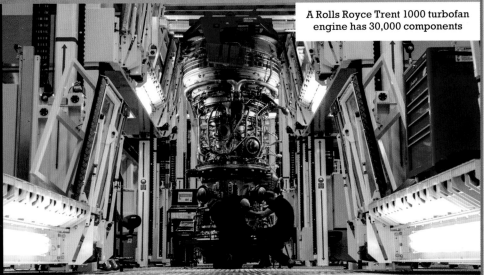
A Rolls Royce Trent 1000 turbofan engine has 30,000 components

Spirit of St. Louis
This monoplane took Charles Lindbergh in 1927 on the world's first solo, non-stop Atlantic crossing.

Powerful engines

Passenger and cargo planes are getting bigger, and though lightweight materials lower overall weight, the aircraft require powerful, reliable engines. They also have to be quiet, use less fuel, and emit less fumes. To assemble one jet engine takes two years; to design and test, five years.

de Havilland Comet
In 1952, this plane started the commercial airline industry, but its reputation was marred by accidents.

The "superjumbo"

In 2007, this was the nickname of the first Airbus A380—the world's largest passenger airplane—ready for service. It can fly at an altitude of 42,999 ft (13,106 m) and has a cruising speed of 559.2 mph (900 kph), and its 9,755.5-mile (15,700-km) range means it can fly non-stop from New Zealand to Dubai.

A wide-body A380 on a long-haul flight

Concorde
The delta-winged Concorde made its first supersonic passenger flight in 1976, and its last in 2003.

Machines in space

Successful space **travel** is the result of millennia of human aspiration and **invention**. Without that first wheel and axle, there would be no Space Shuttle—its 2.5 million **moving** parts making it the most **complex** machine ever built. And without machines like the **telescope** and observatories that reveal what lies **beyond** our skies, there would be no footprints on the Moon. Space exploration was controlled by governments until, in **2001**, a space tourist, Dennis Tito, stepped onto the **International Space Station** (ISS). Since then, the **idea** that one day we could all go to space has taken hold.

Voyager 2 has been in space for over 39 years and is still going.

Apollo 15's Lunar Rover Vehicle had seatbelts, four-wheel drive, and a gyroscope for navigation

Did you know?

The Crawlers are NASA's mobile launcher platforms. They are 131.2 by 114.8 feet (40 by 35 m) in size, 26.2 feet (8 m) high and move on eight tracks. A laser system keeps them level even on a slope.

Space submarines

To explore the lakes and under the ice of Saturn's moons, NASA plans to send a submarine and cryobot in the launch vehicle. Cryobots are heated devices that can penetrate ice.

First into space

In 1949 a V-2-WAC rocket became the first human-made object in space when it reached an altitude of 244.2 miles (393 km).

The Endeavour Space Shuttle takes off in 2011

Space Shuttles

NASA's five shuttles did 135 missions, mostly two weeks in length, from 1979 to 2011. They traveled more than 536.9 million miles (864 million km)! A shuttle has 2.5 million parts and over 1,600 valves and connectors. Less than 10 minutes after launch, its speed is 17,398.4 miles (28,000 km) an hour.

Building in space

Construction of the ISS began in 1998 and, through 2016, it was home to 226 astronauts. Among all its outstanding engineering was Canadarm, known as "ISS's right hand." This robotic arm can maneuver cargo, make repairs, secure astronauts, and even dislodge dangerous ice from a Space Shuttle.

Canadarm 2 captures a spacecraft loaded with supplies for the ISS

Fact file

Machines in orbit

Many machines have been sent to the ISS or taken by the astronauts in their personal luggage.

3D printer
Set up in the ISS in 2014 and still there, its first job was to print a set of tools especially for the ISS.

Toy sets space record
A Buzz Lightyear action figure set an "astronaut" endurance record of 467 days onboard the ISS.

Humanoid robot
Kirobo was made to amuse astronauts in the ISS. The 13.4-inch (34-cm) robot spent 18 months in space.

Musical instrument
The first in space, in 1984, was a saxophone. It was followed by a guitar, flute, keyboard, and bagpipe.

Lunar truck

This bit of equipment is intended for use in NASA's first return mission to the Moon in 50 years. Moving in a crab-like way, each of its six pairs of wheels rotates 360 degrees, letting the truck drive in any direction and out of craters. The addition of a pressurized cabin would make day-long Moon excursions possible.

Testing a lunar truck prototype in the Lunar Yard at NASA

Domestic machines

Machines that **increase** productivity were widespread in factories and agriculture **long** before labor-saving appliances were found in the **home**. Housework was done by women until the 1920s and was not valued, so machines for housework were **not** a priority. Wealthy households had some **powered** machines in the 1800s, but most people used elbow grease to wash, **clean**, and cook until the 1930s. The labor-saving machines then most in **demand** were the vacuum cleaner, washing machine, and **kettle**. These same machines still appear on current lists of greatest **inventions**.

Did you know?

Cragside, England, in 1868, was the first house in the world with electricity. Lights, an elevator, and labor-saving devices were driven by water-powered generators.

Mounted to this 1940s washing machine are hand-turned rollers to squeeze the water from wet clothes

In **1900,** doing **housework** was a **full-time job;** today, it **takes just** 18 hours a **week.**

"Puffing Billy"

This was the nickname of an early vacuum cleaner. It had a gasoline engine and was moved house to house on a horse-drawn cart.

Washing day

The first washing machine wasn't a machine—it was a wooden scrubbing board. The first computerized (microchip) washing machine appeared in 1978.

Sewing machine

Clothes were sewn with needle and thread until the mid-1800s, when the first practical domestic sewing machines appeared. Turning a wheel or pressing a treadle with a foot activated a threaded needle to move up and down and pick up a second thread under the fabric. In 1889, the electric sewing machine was invented.

Electricity

Electric appliances started to appear in the mid-1800s, 80 years before household electricity supply was common. Oddly, the electric doorbell was invented before useful appliances like irons, kettles, or stoves. The first toaster, El Tosto, appeared in 1905.

The first practical domestic sewing machine

A selection of electric-powered devices of the 1800s

Electric kettle

Electric hot water jug

Electric cooker

Electric hotplate

Domestic robots

The first robot (1928) could do little more than move its head and arms, and the original remote-controlled machine was a torpedo boat! Today, a robot will vacuum the floor, then drag itself to a charging station. By 2050, autonomous (operated without human control) robots will be doing all household chores.

Robotic vacuum cleaners have built-in cameras or smart sensor technology

Fact file

Space race in the home

NASA developed 2,000 products and machines for space travel that are now used in homes, medicine, agriculture, and industry.

Laptops
These started as SPOCS—Shuttle Portable Onboard Computers—for NASA missions in 1983.

Cordless power tools
The first battery-powered tool, a drill, was developed so astronauts could collect Moon rock samples.

Smoke detectors
Toxic fume and smoke detectors were invented for use on the orbiting Skylab in the early 1970s.

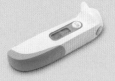

Ear thermometers
These use the infrared technology invented by NASA to measure the temperature of stars.

Machines of war

Military machines have always had two functions: to propel a projectile or to provide **protection**. The bow is a lever that releases an arrow, and a launcher rocket propels a **missile**. **Chariots**, like armored tanks, protected and provided an advantage to their occupants. But since **1916**, advances in physics, **chemistry**, and engineering made land, sea, and air military machines more devastating than ever. The **vehicles** and their weaponry **travel** faster and farther, and can cause harm without detection, unmanned and thousands of miles from a **target**.

The first **submarine** had **30 minutes of air** for its **passenger—** the **latest** can stay **submerged** for **25 years!**

NASA's experimental X-43A travels at 7,000 miles (11,265 km) per hour—the current speed record for a jet aircraft

Facts and figures

Military machines that save lives

Medical dummies
Lifelike robotic mannequins with sensors and computers are being used to train military medical staff. The dummies can exhibit symptoms like sweating and replicate heart attacks and combat injuries. The dummy's condition—from critical to stable—can be altered from the trainer's computer to suit any specific training situation.

Robots
Robots, like Packbot, that are controlled remotely by a joystick investigate dangerous locations or packages while soldiers stay at a safe distance.

Autonomous vehicle
In development is an autonomous miniroller with 12 wheels, sensors, and radar that will survey if a road is free of explosive devices before vehicles use the road.

Did you know?

Taranis, named after a god of thunder, is a 39.4-foot (12-m)-long, supersonic drone for combat and surveillance. In autonomous mode, it "thinks" and navigates itself.

Gatling gun

In 1862, Gatling invented a hand-cranked gun that changed combat. This machine gun could fire 200 rounds a minute; today's versions fire 6,000 rounds a minute.

Turtle submarine

This was the first military sub (1775), a 9.8-foot (3-m)-long wooden shell-like pod, powered by a hand-turned propeller.

Pushing the envelope

In 1948, the Bell X-1 broke the speed of sound, reaching 700.3 mph (1,127 kph). The pilot, Chuck Yaeger, named the orange rocket-powered craft "Glamorous Glennis" for his wife. At the speed of sound, shockwaves form around the airplane, causing the explosive sound of a sonic boom.

A Bell X-1 test flight a year before it broke the sound barrier

A 1958 T-55 tank churning dust with its five-wheeled tracks

Armored tanks

The first tank was used on a battlefield in 1916 to get to the enemy's frontlines. Protected by thick sheets of metal armor and with weaponry, a tank and its caterpillar tracks can cope with rough terrain and steep slopes. The heaviest tank weighs 207 US tons (188 metric tons)!

Transport robots

Autonomous robots to do the job once done by packhorses—carrying equipment—are in development . One version can carry gear weighing 339.5 pounds (154 kg), run at 3.7 miles (6 km) per hour, cope with rough and steep terrain, snow, and water, and navigate autonomously around obstacles.

AlphaDog, a prototype "legged squad support system"

Fact file

Feats of engineering

Military craft are designed from the ground up for a specific function and engineered for safety and total reliability.

Vertical takeoff
Movable nozzles direct the Harrier's thrust for vertical takeoff and forward and backward flight.

Attack helicopters
Also known as gunships, aircraft like the Apache are fitted with machine guns, rockets, and missiles.

Stealth aircraft
The Blackbird SR-71 is not only one of the world's fastest aircraft, it is also invisible to detection by radar.

Supersonic interceptors
These use their speed—the MiG 25 could do 1,985.4 miles (3,200 km) per hour—to foil enemy air missions.

Construction and mining

As human **civilization** developed, tools were made so that permanent structures could be **built**. A collection of a few dwellings grew into a community and eventually into a **city**, and at each stage tools and machines were **invented** to meet the challenge. As machines became more complex, **humans** tackled ever more ambitious **projects**—pyramids, forts, cathedrals, wells, and aqueducts. But it was the **shift** from human and animal muscle to **powered** machines that made skyscrapers, mines, underwater tunnels, vast dams, and 102.5-mile (165-km)-long bridges **possible**.

Facts and figures

Toolboxes through the ages

Stone Age: small tools made of stone, bone, or wood, such as axes, hammers, chisels, and stone drills.

Copper/Bronze ages: metal tools such as saws and carving tools, as well as rolling logs and sleds.

Iron Age: handplanes, hammers, and drilling tools, as well as wooden cranes, pulleys, scaffolds, and ramps.

Roman period: waterwheels, sawmills, and stronger cranes.

Middle Ages: machines to drive piles into the ground for foundations, and machine tools.

1600s–1800s: steel tools, spirit levels, carpenter's squares, and threaded nuts.

Industrial Revolution: circular saws, claw hammers, and nails.

The first earthmoving machines were the digging stick and the shovel.

Bucket-wheel excavators are the largest land vehicles ever built

Did you know?

To move 66 huge radio telescopes up to the site of the world's largest astronomy project at Atacama, Chile, two 28-wheeled, 65.6-foot (20-m)-long transporters were used.

Powered drill

A jackhammer, also called a pneumatic drill, breaks up rocks or pavement. It is a dangerously loud machine.

Wrecking ball

Until the 1960s, demolition used a 12,125.4-pound (5,500-kg) metal ball that was released from a crane's holding cable to swing, like a pendulum, and smash its target.

Size and weight can limit a giant excavator's speed

Bucket-wheel excavators can dig an area the size of a soccer field to a depth of 108.3 ft (33 m) a day! The largest of these has 5 operators, weighs 17,253.4 US tons (15,652 metric tons) and is 738.2 ft (225 m) long. The wheel is 68.9 ft (21 m) across, and each of the 20 buckets holds 15 trailer-loads of coal.

Fact file

Big machines

Huge construction projects need big machines to excavate deep pits, transport materials, or lift structural components to dizzying heights.

Belaz 75710 dumper truck
As tall as a two-story building, its tires are 13.8 ft (4.2 m) high, and it can carry 496 US tons (450 metric tons) per load.

Bucyrus RH400 shovel
This 19.7-foot (6-m) shovel can load 1,765.7 cubic feet (50 cubic m) of earth—the size of a one-car garage.

Boring Bertha

The Bertha tunnel-boring machine (TBM) is far from boring—its cutting head is 57.4 ft (17.5 m) in diameter, and the processing section behind it is 324.8 ft (99 m) in length. To get into the launch pit, a TBM is lowered bit-by-bit and then assembled in the pit. Bertha can cut away 282.5 cubic ft (8 cubic m) of rock for each inch (2.5 cm) traveled.

There are 700 steel cutter blades on Bertha's head

Big lifters

Cranes are machines that lift, lower, and move loads with pulleys and cables. Tower cranes are fixed in position and can reach 262.5 ft (80 m). Mobile cranes are mounted on wheeled vehicles. There are even floating cranes for marine construction.

A Liebherr mobile crane lifts an 82-ton Airbus A300

Komatzu D575A bulldozer
This superdozer can push rock and soil weighing 346,125.8 pounds (157,000 kg) with its 23-foot (7-m)-wide blade.

Bridge-building machine
The 328-foot (100-m)-long "Iron Monster" lays beams between bridge pillars without the use of cranes.

Science and technology

The machine has come a **long** way since the first astrological prediction instrument of **200 BCE**, the microscope of the 1500s, and the mechanical calculator of the 1600s. In **modern** machines, **digital** electronics drive the engineering, with a tiny silicon chip at the **heart** of even the most massive machines. In 2009, "Adam" became the **first** machine to make a scientific discovery. This "robot scientist" automatically **carried** out research into the genes of an organism. But when not doing breakthrough **science**, machines are smashing protons, exploring exploding **stars**, and doing surgery!

The Hadron Collider smashes the universe's smallest particles.

The magnet inside Large Hadron Coll[i...] detector measure[s] 42.7 by 19.7 fee[t] (13 by 6 m)

Ancient computer
The Antikythera of 200 BCE had 30 meshed bronze gears and was used to predict astrological events like eclipses.

IceCube telescope
This detects particles from exploding stars and other violent events. The telescope system covers 0.39 square miles (1 sq km) of ice to a depth of 0.62 miles (1 km)!

Did you know?
The Z-Machine is an X-ray generator. It is so powerful it is housed in a tank of water and oil. It can propel an object from zero to 75,807.3 miles (122,000 km) per hour in a second.

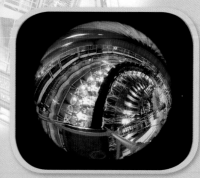

Surgical robot

A robot performs the surgery under the control of surgeons who manipulate the robot's instrument arms remotely. Surgical robots can make the smallest incisions without tremor, and their "wrists" rotate further than the human hand. Three million robot surgeries have been done to date.

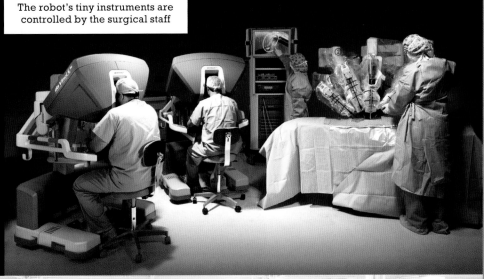

The robot's tiny instruments are controlled by the surgical staff

Titan industrial robots in a car assembly plant

Industrial robots

In 1962, the first industrial robot, Unimate, moved diecastings to an assembly line and spot welded them. Forty years later, there were 2 million industrial robots doing assembly, packaging, picking, lifting, and testing. The most advanced versions make "decisions," move independently, handle things skillfully, and communicate.

Atomic clocks

Clocks that make GPS navigation and the Internet work are atomic clocks. In these, one second is 9,192,631,770 vibrations of a caesium atom. They lose only 0.0001 of a second a day. Optical clocks are accurate to half a second over 65 million years!

A strontium-ion optical clock— the most accurate machine in the world

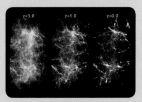

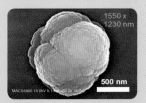

Clever machines

The main result of the Information Age is that **humans** can do more by doing less. Many of the **repetitive**, labor-intensive, and often dangerous jobs done by **people** in the Industrial Age are now performed by computerized machines. The **latest** of these machines can do things that exceed the **abilities** of humans. The world's **largest** supercomputer, Sunway TaihuLight, can do **93 petaflops**. A petaflop is a thousand trillion calculations a second. This machine fills a warehouse, but an **army** of microscopic **robots** could be the world's future labor force.

Did you know?

Charles Babbage's first mechanical computer in 1822 was a calculator. His 1832 Analytical Engine, which used punch cards, could perform any mathematical calculation.

The **Industrial Age** gave us machines, and the **Information Age**, really smart machines.

This nanobot, shown on a pin head, could target a drug to where it is needed in the body

Fast-food robot

This multi-tasking robot can make and shape a proper hamburger and then cook and flip it in 10 seconds!

What's a nanobot?

This is a microscopically-sized robot that could fit inside a human cell. Though nanobots do not yet exist, microscopic nanoparticles make fabrics stain resistant.

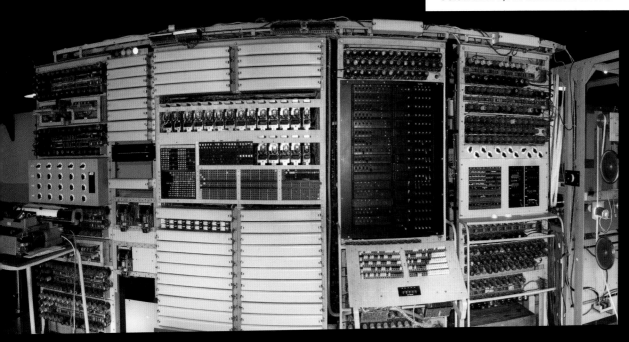

Punched tape being read by Colossus at 5,000 characters a second

Birth of digital

Colossus, designed by Tommy Flowers in 1943–45, was the first programmable, digital, electronic computer. It had hundreds of switches and plugs and over 1,700 valves. Colossus could only crack enemy codes; the first general purpose machine was the Electronic Numerical Integrator and Computer (ENIAC).

Soccer robots

Squads of robots have learned to play soccer. They can plan their own moves, get around the field, kick the red ball, and know when a player is near them, but take a dive, or fall over, a lot. There is even a league for these players: the RoboCup.

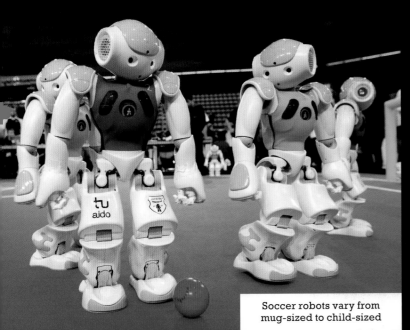

Soccer robots vary from mug-sized to child-sized

The 3D revolution

A 3D printer can make almost anything—from a toy to a whole car! Things once made in factories can be printed at home. A 3D printer slices a digitized image of the object into thousands of micro-thin slices, then prints each layer, starting from the bottom, using melted filaments of plastic.

Using colored plastic filaments, 3D-printed pears look good enough to eat

A 3D-printed hand is so detailed it can be read by a fingerprint scanner

Fact file

3D printed machines

The first 3D-printed object on Earth was a cup in 1981. In space, the first object was a "Made in Space—NASA" nameplate.

Strati car

This car was printed in 2014 in 44 hours using lightweight carbon fiber; car-printing factories may soon be set up.

Miniature power tool

Lance Abernathy's 3D-printed toolkit includes the world's smallest working circular saw and drill.

Artificial limbs

3D-printed prosthetics, like a hand, can be made inexpensively in a day to exactly suit the wearer.

Drones

Not only can a quadcopter drone be 3D printed, you can also purchase and customize the printing files.

Machines for fun

Not all machines make something **useful** or are intended to save time or **effort**. Some machines take away the need for manual labor; others give us ways to spend our **leisure** time. One day, machines with artificial intelligence **(AI)** and human-like emotions may do our **thinking** for us. Advances in technology, or machines based on scientific **knowledge**, could endanger many jobs. In **sport**, many decisions are already made by computers. But there's plenty of time to make engines from building **blocks**, ride roller coasters and man-made waves, and have **fun** on arcade machines.

Did you know?

Ferris wheels are named for their inventor, George Washington Ferris. The High Roller in Las Vegas, Nevada, is the world's tallest at 548 feet (167 m). It takes 30 minutes per revolution.

A computer-generated blueprint for a working, LEGO®-built, attack robot

AI machines of the future will be able to play games and solve the world's greatest problems.

Made by robots

LEGO® factory robots make 36 million pieces a year, from the precision injection molding to the sorting and packing.

Surf's up

Small waves in swimming pools are made with rotating paddlewheels or by blasting air over the water. For much larger waves, a plunger forces water into a pool and sucks it out again.

Roller coasters

Early roller coasters were downhill rides on wheeled sleds and coal carts on mine tracks. The first oval track ride, mounted on an elevated frame, appeared in 1885 in Coney Island, NY. Its open carts reached 11.8 miles (19 km) per hour. Today's fastest coaster hits 149.8 miles (241 km) per hour on a 1.4-mile (2.2-km) track.

Roller coaster train wheels clamp to each side of the track—top, sides, and bottom

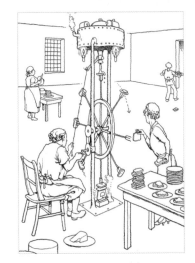

The fire-breathing Tradinno is the world's largest walking robot

Glue, dripped onto a roller, picks up litter in this Heath Robinson machine

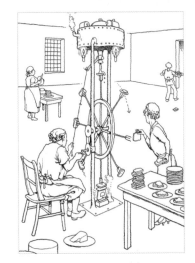

Heath Robinson's humorous contraption for making grilled cheese sandwiches

Mechatronic beasts

Mechanical, electronic, computer, and optical engineering and information technology are combined in mechatronics. Anti-lock brakes, robots, and computer disk drives are examples of mechatronic engineering, as are many of the very realistic-looking beasts seen in films.

Crazy machines

William Heath Robinson (1872–1944) was an illustrator who produced humorous cartoons of bizarre machines powered by steaming kettles and worked by madcap systems of ropes, levers, pulleys, and more. His name, Heath Robinson, has become the nickname for any badly functioning device.

Fact file

Coin-operated machines

Once totally mechanical, today's retail, game, and arcade machines are loaded with electronics and integrated circuits.

Claw machines

The claw is controlled by the player to position it over a prize, then it is lowered to grab the prize.

Penny drop machines

Players win when their coin falls onto the moving trays, causing other coins to fall into an open basket.

Pinball machines

Two flippers, controlled by the player, propel a ball around the game to hit the point-scoring targets.

Vending machines

These machines unlock a drawer or door or release the selected item into an open tray after payment.

Glossary

Agriculture
Another word for farming—growing crops and rearing animals for food or other products.

Astronomy
The science of space, celestial objects, and the universe around us.

Autonomous
Something that has the freedom to act independently, without control by others.

Aviation
The flying of aircraft, or the design, development, and production of a machine that can fly.

Axle
A rod that passes through the center of a wheel.

Carbon zero
When the amount of carbon emitted (e.g., by a country's industrial activities) equals the same amount as the carbon replaced by renewable energy, or that which is absorbed by planted trees.

Combustion
The burning of something, such as a fuel.

Combustion engine
An engine that gets its mechanical power from the combustion of a fuel.

Commercial
With a purpose of making a profit.

Compound
Something made up of many parts or elements.

Condenser
A container used for changing gas or vapor into a liquid.

Cultivate
The use of land for crops or gardening—preparing the land and growing crops on that land.

Excavator
A large, powerful machine designed for digging and moving earth.

Extraction
The action of moving or taking something out, especially by force.

Fell
The action of cutting down a tree.

Flywheel
A heavy, revolving wheel used in a machine.

Force
Strength or energy used in the action of movement. When one object pushes or pulls on another object, it is a force.

Forerunner
Something that precedes (comes before) the development of something else.

Hydroelectric
A form of electricity powered by the movement of water.

Industrial Revolution
The rapid development of industry in the 18th and 19th centuries, made possible by the use of machine power.

Innovation
Introducing new methods, ideas, or products—to change something.

Locomotive
A railway vehicle that pulls trains.

Mechatronics
Technology that combines mechanical engineering with electronics. A robot is an example of a mechatronic creation.

Nanoparticle
A tiny object, or particle, between 1 and 100 nanometers in size. A nanometer is equal to one billionth of a meter.

Petaflop
A measurement of computer speed.

Pressurized
An environment in which high pressure is maintained—the pressure within the environment is higher than outside.

Productivity
A level of being productive—which is the ability to produce a large amount of something within a timeframe.

Proton
An extremely small particle that cannot be seen with the naked eye and has a positive charge to it.

Scavenging
Searching for and collecting objects among discarded waste.

Shockwave
An area of very high pressure moving through a narrow region, traveling through a medium such as air or water. Usually caused by an explosion or by an object moving faster than the speed of sound.

Sonic boom
A loud, explosive noise created by the shockwaves of an aircraft that is traveling faster than the speed of sound.

Submersible
A boat or craft that is designed to work under water (submerged).

Surveillance
Another word for keeping a close watch over a person or place.

Sustainable energy
Energy that is sustainable over time—such as energy powered by wind, sun, or water.

Terrain
Another word for a stretch of land.

Trans-Antarctic
Another way of saying "across the Antarctic."

Treadle
A lever that is operated by the foot and powers a machine.

Index